MW00998593

This book was designed, produced, and published by Landauer Books
A division of Landauer Corporation
12251 Maffitt Road, Cumming, Iowa 50061

President: Jeramy Lanigan Landauer
Vice President: Becky Johnston
Managing Editor: Marlene Hemberger Heuertz
Art Director: Laurel Albright
Concept and Creative Director: Lynette Jensen
Photographer: Craig Anderson
Photostyling: Lynette Jensen and Margaret Sindelar
Technical Writer: Sue Bahr
Graphics Technician: Stewart Cott
Technical Illustrator: Lisa Kirchoff

We also wish to thank the support staff of the Thimbleberries® Design Studio:
Sherry Husske, Virginia Brodd, Renae Ashwill, Ardelle Paulson, Kathy Lobeck,
Carla Plowman, Julie Jergens, Pearl Baysinger, Tracy Schrantz, Leone Rusch, and Julie Borg.

This book is printed on acid-free paper.

Printed in China 10 9 8 7 6 5 4 3 2 1

My
Quilting
Journal

Keeping a journal about your quilts...

Every quilt has a story to tell and holds special memories for its maker.

In this journal celebrating memories and milestones, quilt designer Lynette Jensen offers you an opportunity to record thoughts, photographs, and swatches of your own favorite quilts—a must-have memory book for every quilter.

In the past, a handmade quilt was a special gift, treasured for a lifetime, and carefully preserved for the next generation. Today, you can carry on that tradition with quilts made to commemorate favorite milestones—from the birth of a new baby to weddings, anniversaries, housewarmings, and even a special birthday. Each theme celebrating a milestone features a quilt designed by Lynette Jensen for Thimbleberries® along with her special memories of the inspiration for designing the quilt. For a starting point in recording your favorite quilts, begin with the themes that have inspired Lynette, and then branch out into recording memories and photographs of quilts that celebrate your own everyday memories.

This journal is conveniently-sized to accommodate a standard 4 x 6-inch photograph or swatches of the fabrics used to make your quilt, and printed on acid-free paper to protect the contents for the future. You'll want to use acid-free tape for securing your photographs and an acid-free pen for recording your memories and thoughts on the lines provided on the following pages. The spiral binding makes it easy to use and fill with memories of your own unique quilts for a treasured book to share with friends, family, and future generations. Enjoy!

From Lynette

Of the hundreds of quilts I've designed down through the years, the ones I recall most vividly are those I made to share with loved ones! Handmade quilts given with love represent every quilter's hope and faith in the future, and what better way to preserve that heritage than with a journal filled with memories of your favorite quilts.

To get you started, throughout the pages of this journal you'll find my thoughts about special occasion quilts I've designed for baby, girls only, boys only, leaving home, wedding, birthday, the four seasons—spring, summer, autumn, and winter—anniversary, housewarming, and my all-time favorite quilt. (If you'd like to make any of these quilts, you'll find the Thimbleberries® patterns sourced in the back of this journal.)

Once your thoughts are flowing, I'm sure you'll be inspired by your favorite quilts to fill the pages of this journal with memories of even more categories of special occasion quilts, limited only by your imagination. And remember, whether your own quilt is made to keep or give to others, the memories it holds will stay in hearts forever! Wishing you more wonderful quilting memories than your heart can hold...

Lynette Jensen

Oh Baby, Baby

My Favorite Quilts

My Favorite Quilts
My Favorite Quilts
My Favorite Quilts

*To me, babies are small reminders of everything pure, simple, clean, and sweet.
In designing a quilt that is a suitable gift for a baby girl or boy, I combined delicate
cotton prints with a soft, cream-colored print fabric for tiny pieced blocks.
The pieced top can easily be enlarged by adding simple borders to the pieced quilt center.*

Place Photo or Fabric Swatches Here

I began this quilt on:

Date: ______________________

I finished this quilt on:

Date: ______________________

Colors and fabrics used:

Quilted with love for:

Name: ______________________

My thoughts about the quilt:

Place Photo or Fabric Swatches Here

I began this quilt on:

Date: ______________________

I finished this quilt on:

Date: ______________________

Colors and fabrics used:

____

____

____

____

____

____

____

____

Quilted with love for:

Name: ______________________

My thoughts about the quilt:

____

____

____

____

____

____

____

____

____

____

____

____

____

____

____

____

Place Photo or Fabric Swatches Here

I began this quilt on:

Date: ______________________

I finished this quilt on:

Date: ______________________

Colors and fabrics used:

____

____

____

____

____

____

____

____

Quilted with love for:

Name: ______________________

My thoughts about the quilt:

____

____

____

____

____

____

____

____

____

____

____

____

____

____

____

____

Place Photo or Fabric Swatches Here

I began this quilt on:

Date: ____________________

I finished this quilt on:

Date: ____________________

Colors and fabrics used:

Quilted with love for:

Name: ____________________

My thoughts about the quilt:

Color Book Garden

My Favorite Quilts

My Favorite Quilts

My Favorite Quilts

My Favorite Quilts

The ideal quilt for transitioning a little girl from the crib to her first "big" bed is one that can still be enjoyed even when she goes off to college! In the years to come, what better reminder of family than a quilt a daughter recalls fondly as having cherished since she was a child. This kind of heirloom-quality quilt will ensure years of enduring memories for that special little girl in your life.

Place Photo or Fabric Swatches Here

I began this quilt on:

Date: ________________________

I finished this quilt on:

Date: ________________________

Colors and fabrics used:

____

____

____

____

____

____

____

____

Quilted with love for:

Name: ________________________

My thoughts about the quilt:

____

____

____

____

____

____

____

____

____

____

____

____

____

____

____

____

Place Photo or Fabric Swatches Here

I began this quilt on:

Date: ______________________

I finished this quilt on:

Date: ______________________

Colors and fabrics used:

____

____

____

____

____

____

____

____

Quilted with love for:

Name: ______________________

My thoughts about the quilt:

____

____

____

____

____

____

____

____

____

____

____

____

____

____

____

____

Place Photo or Fabric Swatches Here

I began this quilt on:

Date: ____________________

I finished this quilt on:

Date: ____________________

Colors and fabrics used:

Quilted with love for:

Name: ____________________

My thoughts about the quilt:

Place Photo or Fabric Swatches Here

I began this quilt on:

Date: ______________________

I finished this quilt on:

Date: ______________________

Colors and fabrics used:

____

____

____

____

____

____

____

____

Quilted with love for:

Name: ______________________

My thoughts about the quilt:

____

____

____

____

____

____

____

____

____

____

____

____

____

____

____

____

Patches & Plaids

My Favorite Quilts

My Favorite Quilts
My Favorite Quilts
My Favorite Quilts

The perfect quilt for transitioning a little boy from the crib to his first "real" bed, is a nine-patch that reminds me of plaid shirts from the forties and the rough and tumble nature of most boys! I chose a quilt block pattern that is not too detailed or fussy and pieced it using cotton prints that will always fit into a masculine room—just right for a boy when he is four and all-too-soon grows up to be 24!

Place Photo or Fabric Swatches Here

I began this quilt on:

Date: ____________________

I finished this quilt on:

Date: ____________________

Colors and fabrics used:

Quilted with love for:

Name: ____________________

My thoughts about the quilt:

Place Photo or Fabric Swatches Here

I began this quilt on:

Date: ____________________

I finished this quilt on:

Date: ____________________

Colors and fabrics used:

Quilted with love for:

Name: ____________________

My thoughts about the quilt:

Place Photo or Fabric Swatches Here

I began this quilt on:

Date: ______________________

I finished this quilt on:

Date: ______________________

Colors and fabrics used:

____

____

____

____

____

____

____

____

Quilted with love for:

Name: ______________________

My thoughts about the quilt:

____

____

____

____

____

____

____

____

____

____

____

____

____

____

____

____

Place Photo or Fabric Swatches Here

I began this quilt on:

Date: ________________________

I finished this quilt on:

Date: ________________________

Colors and fabrics used:

Quilted with love for:

Name: ________________________

My thoughts about the quilt:

GARDEN SCAPE

My Favorite Quilts

My Favorite Quilts

My Favorite Quilts

My Favorite Quilts

It seems like all too soon our children are ready to leave home, and what better way to send them off than with a special quilt that is a reminder of hearth and home? I used the log cabin pattern for this "leaving home" quilt because traditionally, the center block represents the light in the window of the cabin that is the center of the home. Taking these feelings with them is as comforting and cozy as this quilt—and one of the best gifts we can give our children.

Place Photo or Fabric Swatches Here

I began this quilt on:

Date: ______________________________

I finished this quilt on:

Date: ______________________________

Colors and fabrics used:

____

____

____

____

____

____

____

____

Quilted with love for:

Name: ______________________________

My thoughts about the quilt:

____

____

____

____

____

____

____

____

____

____

____

____

____

____

____

____

Place Photo or Fabric Swatches Here

I began this quilt on:

Date: ____________________

I finished this quilt on:

Date: ____________________

Colors and fabrics used:

Quilted with love for:

Name: ____________________

My thoughts about the quilt:

Place Photo or Fabric Swatches Here

I began this quilt on:

Date: ______________________

I finished this quilt on:

Date: ______________________

Colors and fabrics used:

____

____

____

____

____

____

____

____

Quilted with love for:

Name: ______________________

My thoughts about the quilt:

____

____

____

____

____

____

____

____

____

____

____

____

____

____

____

____

Place Photo or Fabric Swatches Here

I began this quilt on:

Date: ______________________

I finished this quilt on:

Date: ______________________

Colors and fabrics used:

____

____

____

____

____

____

____

____

Quilted with love for:

Name: ______________________

My thoughts about the quilt:

____

____

____

____

____

____

____

____

____

____

____

____

____

____

____

____

Wedding Basket

My Favorite Quilts

My Favorite Quilts

My Favorite Quilts

My Favorite Quilts

This appliqué basket block set on point was replicated from a quilt made by my husband Neil's Aunt Dema for his parents' 1939 wedding. I adapted the design using Thimbleberries® fabrics for a wedding quilt given from Neil and me to our daughter Kerry and son-in-law, Trevor for their 1999 wedding. It was interesting to note that 30 years later, Aunt Dema, who had faded into family history was the subject of conversation regarding Kerry's grandmother's wedding quilt. I am always amazed at how a simple quilt can so easily connect the generations.

Place Photo or Fabric Swatches Here

I began this quilt on:

Date: ______________________________

I finished this quilt on:

Date: ______________________________

Colors and fabrics used:

Quilted with love for:

Name: ______________________________

My thoughts about the quilt:

Place Photo or Fabric Swatches Here

I began this quilt on:

Date: ______________________

I finished this quilt on:

Date: ______________________

Colors and fabrics used:

____

____

____

____

____

____

____

____

Quilted with love for:

Name: ______________________

My thoughts about the quilt:

____

____

____

____

____

____

____

____

____

____

____

____

____

____

____

Place Photo or Fabric Swatches Here

I began this quilt on:

Date: ______________________

I finished this quilt on:

Date: ______________________

Colors and fabrics used:

____

____

____

____

____

____

____

____

Quilted with love for:

Name: ______________________

My thoughts about the quilt:

____

____

____

____

____

____

____

____

____

____

____

____

____

____

____

____

Place Photo or Fabric Swatches Here

I began this quilt on:

Date: ____________________________

I finished this quilt on:

Date: ____________________________

Colors and fabrics used:

Quilted with love for:

Name: ____________________________

My thoughts about the quilt:

My Favorite Quilts
My Favorite Quilts
Party Mix
My Favorite Quilts
My Favorite Quilts

A quilt with big, bright blocks is the perfect complement to any birthday party—regardless of how many candles are on the cake. The explosion of color in the blocks reminds me of balloons, confetti, ribbons, and wrapping paper. I designed this straightforward quilt to be as fast and fun to make as it is festive, just the right ingredients for any birthday celebration!

Place Photo or Fabric Swatches Here

I began this quilt on:

Date: ______________________________

I finished this quilt on:

Date: ______________________________

Colors and fabrics used:

____

____

____

____

____

____

____

____

Quilted with love for:

Name: ______________________________

My thoughts about the quilt:

____

____

____

____

____

____

____

____

____

____

____

____

____

____

____

____

Place Photo or Fabric Swatches Here

I began this quilt on:

Date: ______________________________

I finished this quilt on:

Date: ______________________________

Colors and fabrics used:

____

____

____

____

____

____

____

____

Quilted with love for:

Name: ______________________________

My thoughts about the quilt:

____

____

____

____

____

____

____

____

____

____

____

____

____

____

____

____

Place Photo or Fabric Swatches Here

I began this quilt on:

Date: ____________________

I finished this quilt on:

Date: ____________________

Colors and fabrics used:

Quilted with love for:

Name: ____________________

My thoughts about the quilt:

Place Photo or Fabric Swatches Here

I began this quilt on:

Date: ____________________

I finished this quilt on:

Date: ____________________

Colors and fabrics used:

Quilted with love for:

Name: ____________________

My thoughts about the quilt:

My Favorite Quilts

My Favorite Quilts

Meadow Lily

My Favorite Quilts

My Favorite Quilts

The colors in this variation of a traditional Irish chain remind me of a field filled with the beginnings of early spring flowers poking their heads above the soil. With just a hint of feathery green, the combination of fabrics offers the promise of even more blooms to come. I find the repeat design visually soothing and relaxing—much like warm sunshine after a gentle spring rain.

Place Photo or Fabric Swatches Here

I began this quilt on:

Date: ______________________

I finished this quilt on:

Date: ______________________

Colors and fabrics used:

____

____

____

____

____

____

____

____

Quilted with love for:

Name: ______________________

My thoughts about the quilt:

____

____

____

____

____

____

____

____

____

____

____

____

____

____

____

____

Place Photo or Fabric Swatches Here

I began this quilt on:

Date: ______________________________

I finished this quilt on:

Date: ______________________________

Colors and fabrics used:

Quilted with love for:

Name: ______________________________

My thoughts about the quilt:

Place Photo or Fabric Swatches Here

I began this quilt on:

Date: ____________________

I finished this quilt on:

Date: ____________________

Colors and fabrics used:

Quilted with love for:

Name: ____________________

My thoughts about the quilt:

Place Photo or Fabric Swatches Here

I began this quilt on:

Date: ______________________

I finished this quilt on:

Date: ______________________

Colors and fabrics used:

____

____

____

____

____

____

____

____

Quilted with love for:

Name: ______________________

My thoughts about the quilt:

____

____

____

____

____

____

____

____

____

____

____

____

____

____

____

____

My Favorite Quilts

My Favorite Quilts

Sunny Side Up

My Favorite Quilts

My Favorite Quilts

For a seasonal quilt that says "summer," a true-Irish chain is as light and airy as a summer breeze. The soft floral border, inspired by the hydrangeas and asters from my cutting garden, speaks of summer flowers and blue skies. A quilt this soft and gentle is the perfect accent for summer evenings spent relaxing in a wicker rocker or on the porch swing.

Place Photo or Fabric Swatches Here

I began this quilt on:

Date: ____________________

I finished this quilt on:

Date: ____________________

Colors and fabrics used:

Quilted with love for:

Name: ____________________

My thoughts about the quilt:

Place Photo or Fabric Swatches Here

I began this quilt on:

Date: ____________________________

I finished this quilt on:

Date: ____________________________

Colors and fabrics used:

Quilted with love for:

Name: ____________________________

My thoughts about the quilt:

Place Photo or Fabric Swatches Here

I began this quilt on:

Date: ______________________

I finished this quilt on:

Date: ______________________

Colors and fabrics used:

____

____

____

____

____

____

____

____

Quilted with love for:

Name: ______________________

My thoughts about the quilt:

____

____

____

____

____

____

____

____

____

____

____

____

____

____

____

Place Photo or Fabric Swatches Here

I began this quilt on:

Date: ____________________

I finished this quilt on:

Date: ____________________

Colors and fabrics used:

My thoughts about the quilt:

Quilted with love for:

Name: ____________________

Leaf Gathering

My Favorite Quilts

My Favorite Quilts
My Favorite Quilts
My Favorite Quilts

All the things I love most about autumn are incorporated into this quilt dedicated to leaf gathering. The multitude of colors represents the layering of leaves in bright hues of brown, green, gold, and red, combined with the warm afternoon sun and cool nights. I'm reminded of everything warm and inviting as I bring the glories of autumn into my home with one simple, but spectacular leaf-filled quilt.

Place Photo or Fabric Swatches Here

I began this quilt on:

Date: ______________________________

I finished this quilt on:

Date: ______________________________

Colors and fabrics used:

____

____

____

____

____

____

____

____

Quilted with love for:

Name: ______________________________

My thoughts about the quilt:

____

____

____

____

____

____

____

____

____

____

____

____

____

____

____

____

Place Photo or Fabric Swatches Here

I began this quilt on:

Date: ______________________

I finished this quilt on:

Date: ______________________

Colors and fabrics used:

____

____

____

____

____

____

____

____

Quilted with love for:

Name: ______________________

My thoughts about the quilt:

____

____

____

____

____

____

____

____

____

____

____

____

____

____

____

____

Place Photo or Fabric Swatches Here

I began this quilt on:

Date: ______________________

I finished this quilt on:

Date: ______________________

Colors and fabrics used:

____

____

____

____

____

____

____

____

Quilted with love for:

Name: ______________________

My thoughts about the quilt:

____

____

____

____

____

____

____

____

____

____

____

____

____

____

____

____

Place Photo or Fabric Swatches Here

I began this quilt on:

Date: ______________________

I finished this quilt on:

Date: ______________________

Colors and fabrics used:

____

____

____

____

____

____

____

____

Quilted with love for:

Name: ______________________

My thoughts about the quilt:

____

____

____

____

____

____

____

____

____

____

____

____

____

____

____

____

Winter Memories

My Favorite Quilts

My Favorite Quilts

My Favorite Quilts

My Favorite Quilts

This cozy scrap quilt is a fond remembrance of the bits and pieces of winter memories we all carry in our hearts. The blocks are brimming with bows, snowflakes and stars, hearts, trees, mittens, gingerbread-and-snowmen, and trimmed with wide plaid borders for a fitting tribute to all the joys of winter fun and festivities.

Place Photo or Fabric Swatches Here

I began this quilt on:

Date: ____________________

I finished this quilt on:

Date: ____________________

Colors and fabrics used:

Quilted with love for:

Name: ____________________

My thoughts about the quilt:

Place Photo or Fabric Swatches Here

I began this quilt on:

Date: ______________________

I finished this quilt on:

Date: ______________________

Colors and fabrics used:

____

____

____

____

____

____

____

____

Quilted with love for:

Name: ______________________

My thoughts about the quilt:

____

____

____

____

____

____

____

____

____

____

____

____

____

____

____

____

Place Photo or Fabric Swatches Here

I began this quilt on:

Date: ______________________

I finished this quilt on:

Date: ______________________

Colors and fabrics used:

____

____

____

____

____

____

____

____

Quilted with love for:

Name: ______________________

My thoughts about the quilt:

____

____

____

____

____

____

____

____

____

____

____

____

____

____

____

____

Place Photo or Fabric Swatches Here

I began this quilt on:

Date: ______________________

I finished this quilt on:

Date: ______________________

Colors and fabrics used:

____

____

____

____

____

____

____

____

Quilted with love for:

Name: ______________________

My thoughts about the quilt:

____

____

____

____

____

____

____

____

____

____

____

____

____

____

____

____

My Favorite Quilts
My Favorite Quilts
Cottage Flower
My Favorite Quilts
My Favorite Quilts

Anniversaries are a lot like the flowers that bloom around a country cottage. When you first begin to plant them in nice, neat borders they are easy to count. After awhile, as the plants grow and multiply, the blossoms blend together in a burst of color. Traditional quilt-making is much the same with flowers in the center "blooming" outward to fill the borders. Like flower-bed borders and quilt-making, so it is, too, with anniversaries that celebrate years of our lives which have gradually blended into a blur of pleasant memories.

Place Photo or Fabric Swatches Here

I began this quilt on:

Date: ________________________

I finished this quilt on:

Date: ________________________

Colors and fabrics used:

Quilted with love for:

Name: ________________________

My thoughts about the quilt:

Place Photo or Fabric Swatches Here

I began this quilt on:

Date: ______________________________

I finished this quilt on:

Date: ______________________________

Colors and fabrics used:

____

____

____

____

____

____

____

____

Quilted with love for:

Name: ______________________________

My thoughts about the quilt:

____

____

____

____

____

____

____

____

____

____

____

____

____

____

____

____

Place Photo or Fabric Swatches Here

I began this quilt on:

Date: ____________________

I finished this quilt on:

Date: ____________________

Colors and fabrics used:

Quilted with love for:

Name: ____________________

My thoughts about the quilt:

Place Photo or Fabric Swatches Here

I began this quilt on:

Date: ______________________

I finished this quilt on:

Date: ______________________

Colors and fabrics used:

____

____

____

____

____

____

____

____

Quilted with love for:

Name: ______________________

My thoughts about the quilt:

____

____

____

____

____

____

____

____

____

____

____

____

____

____

____

____

STAR & CHAIN

My Favorite Quilts

My Favorite Quilts

My Favorite Quilts

My Favorite Quilts

For an heirloom housewarming quilt, I chose the traditional star and chain because it is built on the foundation of a very old pattern—a variation of the carpenter's wheel. To me it is important to establish a home on the foundation of timeless traditions such as commitment, trust, honor, and hard work. Through the years I have devoted myself to making harmony the heart of our home. Recently, our son-in-law paid me a great compliment. He said, "I love this house because it always hugs you back!"

Place Photo or Fabric Swatches Here

I began this quilt on:

Date: __________

I finished this quilt on:

Date: __________

Colors and fabrics used:

Quilted with love for:

Name: __________

My thoughts about the quilt:

Place Photo or Fabric Swatches Here

I began this quilt on:

Date: ______________________________

I finished this quilt on:

Date: ______________________________

Colors and fabrics used:

____

____

____

____

____

____

____

____

Quilted with love for:

Name: ______________________________

My thoughts about the quilt:

____

____

____

____

____

____

____

____

____

____

____

____

____

____

____

____

Place Photo or Fabric Swatches Here

I began this quilt on:

Date: ______________________

I finished this quilt on:

Date: ______________________

Colors and fabrics used:

____

____

____

____

____

____

____

____

Quilted with love for:

Name: ______________________

My thoughts about the quilt:

____

____

____

____

____

____

____

____

____

____

____

____

____

____

____

____

Place Photo or Fabric Swatches Here

I began this quilt on:

Date: ____________________

I finished this quilt on:

Date: ____________________

Colors and fabrics used:

____
____
____
____
____
____
____
____

Quilted with love for:

Name: ____________________

My thoughts about the quilt:

____
____
____
____
____
____
____
____
____
____
____
____
____
____
____

Mountain Stars

My Favorite Quilts

My Favorite Quilts

My Favorite Quilts

My Favorite Quilts

I chose this quilt for my all-time favorite because many elements of a truly wonderful quilt come together—in the traditional geometric shapes of the star motifs, the numerous prints radiating out from the center to the borders in a pattern of lights and darks, and the use of color which makes it appear far more complex than it really is. To me, the success of a great quilt design can be judged by how much work it looks like you put into it, when in reality it was quite simple to create a stunning quilt!

Place Photo or Fabric Swatches Here

I began this quilt on:

Date: ______________________

I finished this quilt on:

Date: ______________________

Colors and fabrics used:

Quilted with love for:

Name: ______________________

My thoughts about the quilt:

Place Photo or Fabric Swatches Here

I began this quilt on:

Date: ______________________

I finished this quilt on:

Date: ______________________

Colors and fabrics used:

____

____

____

____

____

____

____

____

Quilted with love for:

Name: ______________________

My thoughts about the quilt:

____

____

____

____

____

____

____

____

____

____

____

____

____

____

____

____

Place Photo or Fabric Swatches Here

I began this quilt on:

Date: ______________________

I finished this quilt on:

Date: ______________________

Colors and fabrics used:

____

____

____

____

____

____

____

____

Quilted with love for:

Name: ______________________

My thoughts about the quilt:

____

____

____

____

____

____

____

____

____

____

____

____

____

____

____

____

Place Photo or Fabric Swatches Here

I began this quilt on:

Date: ______________________

I finished this quilt on:

Date: ______________________

Colors and fabrics used:

Quilted with love for:

Name: ______________________

My thoughts about the quilt:

Place Photo or Fabric Swatches Here

I began this quilt on:

Date: ____________________

I finished this quilt on:

Date: ____________________

Colors and fabrics used:

Quilted with love for:

Name: ____________________

My thoughts about the quilt:

Place Photo or Fabric Swatches Here

I began this quilt on:

Date: ____________________

I finished this quilt on:

Date: ____________________

Colors and fabrics used:

____

____

____

____

____

____

____

____

Quilted with love for:

Name: ____________________

My thoughts about the quilt:

____

____

____

____

____

____

____

____

____

____

____

____

____

____

____

____

Place Photo or Fabric Swatches Here

I began this quilt on:

Date: ______________________

I finished this quilt on:

Date: ______________________

Colors and fabrics used:

____

____

____

____

____

____

____

____

Quilted with love for:

Name: ______________________

My thoughts about the quilt:

____

____

____

____

____

____

____

____

____

____

____

____

____

____

____

Sources

Lynette Jensen's designs for the quilts in this Quilting Journal are available from her Thimbleberries® line of books and patterns, or from Rodale Books. Please call 800/587-3944 to order a catalog, or for more information about obtaining patterns for the quilts shown below.

About Lynette Jensen

Expressing her creativity through quilting, Lynette discovered that by designing her own line of coordinating prints, solids, and plaids she could get exactly what she needed for her growing collection of pieced patchwork. A licensing agreement signed with RJR Fashion Fabrics in 1993 has resulted in an expansive line of fabrics anchored by her signature Paintbox Collection.

Known and respected throughout the quilting world for her Thimbleberries® line of fabrics, Lynette has created an enduring collection of coordinates in a rich palette of country colors that literally spans the seasons.

Lynette combines traditional quilt patterns with an appealing array of appliquéd vines, berries, and blossoms. The result is a charming blend of blocks and borders with soft touches of country color reminiscent of America's more tranquil past.

Her fabric designs have so much appeal that Lynette's design studio, located in a 100-year-old building with original tin ceilings and hardwood floors in downtown Hutchinson, Minnesota, has become a destination for Thimbleberries® enthusiasts who visit from around the world. Main Street Cotton Shop, an independent full-service quilting shop located on the main level of the Thimbleberries® building, currently stocks the entire line of Thimbleberries® patterns, books, fabrics, and quilts.

For Lynette, a Minnesota native and graduate of the University of Minnesota with a degree in Home Economics, the Thimbleberries® design studio and office is a short walk from the home she shares with husband Neil. The spacious studio, filled with antiques and quilts on display, is a wonderful, open, bright spot from which to work and create each day.

In this serene place, surrounded by friends and family, Lynette Jensen designs fabrics and quilts and develops classic country decorating themes which express her unique gift for making harmony the heart of the home.